DIE OR
LIVE TRYING

DIE OR
LIVE TRYING

Taru Thompson

For Rockaway Collegiate High School Class of 2016

10% of all profits from this book will be donated to the Legacy Scholarship Fund for Rockaway Collegiate High School and Williamsburg Charter High School.

A poem doesn't do everything for you. You are supposed to go on with your thinking. You are supposed to enrich the other person's poem with your extensions, your uniquely personal understandings, thus making the poem serve you.

~Gwendolyn Brooks, "Song of Winnie"

Contents

Nouns, Adjectives and Verbs

in the wide world of poetry
what gets your nouns pumping more

~adjectives or verbs~

can you transition
    using only prepositions and an hourglass
or do figures remind you of mirrors
    and mirrors only of hate
what have you seen (in any reflection) that keeps you dripping?
there are thousands
no, millions
slipping through the same crack
    can you feel their coarse caress in the mass exodus?
        would it matter if you did?

for some, nouns are enough company
    adjectives only describe the dream
    and verbs tell you how to get there
but nouns are the shoreline
        and time is the wave gradually pumping you there

Rah

there's something profound in isolation
a single syllable pronounced itself in repetition

Rah   Rah   Rah   Rah

listen,
and you will find exaltation in its echo
a raising up of the mundane

Rah

after so many times
   it will develop its own character
      its own tone

Rah

pride will soon follow
solitary; it will grow its own meaning
   learn to stand alone
sentence structure will fall to the wayside
as self-realization ensues

  in time, others too will understand
this is the goal of all syllables
     of all lone things
to be understood
   and thus
        to be validated

Apples to Apples

I remember 3rd grade
       Ms. Morrow's class
              Apples to Apples
      the word was lovable

I scampered through cards incredulous
who is Marilyn Monroe
and how is she lovable?
I chose Buzz Lightyear

I remember the judge
bobbing for apples
      Ambrosias
         Autumn Golds
she read them aloud
1950s. Robin Hood. Blood.

Blood?!?

we all laughed, a vampire in our midst
  all but Damon
      Damon who pleaded
It's true. The only time Daddy kisses Mommy is after he makes her bleed.

see, for Damon
love was pain's bitter aftertaste
in a house
where kisses were apologies and arguments were whispers
where mice and toy soldiers gossiped Louis' trumpet

love was pain's bitter aftertaste

in a house
where monsters roamed the halls as Goku huddled in fear
where wishlists were Pokeballs
because a dark cell is solace
no red, just rest

for Damon
love was pain's bitter aftertaste
and Listerine wasn't shit
you could keep love to yourself

I remember that day
Ms. Morrow gave Damon a Granny Smith
not because blood was loveable
but because Damon was

so now
whenever I see apples
I think of blood
  & Ms. Morrow
    & Damon
      & love
   and I pray
for all the monsters in the hallways
for their victims
and for all the Gokus still under the bed
that in their own way
they find Pokeballs

Open Letter From A Mother

Child,
there is greatness in your lineage
I won't trace every root for you
they're too nappy
Lord knows this tree been grown in some shit soil
beady with miseducation
southern fried and fatty
but there was greatness here
still is
set in North Carolina cotton fields
we had no business
breaking mason jars
at the foot of the Empire
but we done that anyway
left the road maps back in the shacks
with our imaginary books
we been tracing streets from memory
for generations now

Child,
don't let the you you've been
keep you from the you you wanna be
but know yourself
can't nobody be nothing 'less they know theyself
you, came from a smooth talker
and a premature adult
an array of bad decisions
but you weren't one of 'em
no.
there is greatness *in* you
I saw it when I swaddled you as a baby
and can't nobody hold it back

'cept the cage it's in

Child,
I pray for you
daily
ask God to bless the seeds you sow
to hold off the reaper another day
you have purpose
I don't know what it is
but you are beyond all of this
beyond the roots
beyond the soil
somewhere between the highest branch
and the sun

when you were born
I looked into your eyes
and I *saw* you
I hope
that when you look up
you see the same

Lava Lamp

He was born into a vacuum
inspired by the light (as all things are)
but given purpose by darkness
the coil that once held him
now the fire under his ass
and so
      he awoke
first breath a y

                       a

                 a

                 a

                       a

                w

              n

that seemed an eternity
this, we call foreshadowing
lethargy became the only air he knew
sleep, his only companion
quickly he learned to move like liquid
to ebb with the tide of time
to flow whenever pushed
and this was his life
a constant state of suspended animation
        never moving unless moved
never acting unless acted upon

I Stole From The Pope

I stole from the pope
a Rubik's Cube
and left behind my poetry
mindlessly shifting patterns
aiming for lines of uniformity
I stumbled upon the mystery of God
lost myself in it
between front right up inverted turns
I slipped into fragmented rainbow squares
old covenant promises flooded my mind
I desperately needed swimming lessons
so I life invested in YouTube
watching algorithms match puzzle pieces for me
I figured: *God is just a massive cube ~ the Kabba*
twist scrambled by human minds
but still solvable with some infinite algorithm
problem: math was never my strong suit

I stole from the pope a holy divine Rubik's Cube
but I cannot stop thinking
about my black and white composition book

Do Trains Dream

Stained glass flashing on my skin
I wanna walk through Broadway Junction completely naked
exposed to the evangelists and sinners both
I wanna roll an L with Jay-Z while blasting the A/C
  I have never hotboxed before
      but summer
     seems like the perfect time for these types of dreams
I call them boxcars
  because they are self-contained but always moving
I am always moving
  but to what end
Canarsie was three stops ago, but this train keeps going
the view is panoramic
I can see my past
   an indistinct fog of Rocky Ways
I can see my future
   a city of dreams- skyscrapers and high-rises
and I have no doubt that I will reach my destination

Even before the F train introduced me to Queens
I was chasing bait at Gallery Place
  a fish in a smaller pond
     I learned my primary colors from the Metro Map
train hopping
from Blue line to Green line to Red line
     I learned to plan in Banneker's City
only then did I trade the Monument for the Empire

Statement: *It is good to have an end to journey toward, but it is the journey that matters in the end**

Reason: *We should not judge people by their peak of excellence, but by the distance they have travelled from where they started* **

My journey has spanned millennia and there is no end in sight
Where are you going?

*Ernest Hemingway Quote
**Henry Ward Beecher Quote

P (Queen)

somewhere between never   and   always
I had a pennyful thought
   that love
is a chance occurrence
flip a coin
and the forces that be
will guide it like your heart:

randomly

in love
nothing is certain
it is a crash course in probability
   you will probably get hurt
but before the die is cast for you
take a roll
it is the greatest gamble you can ever know

Can I Live

spin records lifelike
symphonically orchestrated
meticulously detailed
every second planned
every hook preordained

can I live?

inside 16 bars
all run tapless by repetition
drunkenly mellowed to flatline
beeped autotune to flatline

can I live?

bass-goded out of speakers
loud more than true
bustling more than brilliant

can I live?

prostituted to product placement
advertised to compromise

can I live?
in records life-like

Can I?

Marginalized

you can find him folded into life's hidden pockets
a side note to the attention seekers
he is a wallflower
sprouting out of a stereo
music helps him grow
he dances in the margins like sketched vines
permanent yet silent
assimilating so well
you barely notice his presence
but at this moment
he is infinite
subtlety infinite
a dull bass at a roaring party
you may not see him
but he is the land that keeps you steady

Let this be your notice:
   he sees you
(he may be quiet)
    but he sees you
and he understands

A Masochist's Escape

I cut my wrists and all that bled out was ink and insecurities
so I bound the gaping holes shut
stitched a smile back on my face
and kept the words in
each vein a gorging river of prose
a couple sonnets I suppose
but there's no rhyme scheme to my madness
my head is scattered with verses
unconnected stanzas that hold weight like scripture
and they all want confirmation
    that's why they bustle and jolt
    and demand their way out

the rage against is too much to hold inside

    so I grip pen and pad
    and scribble like mad
there's deliverance in their escape
no matter how it comes
I will bleed out on this page
and it will be the sweetest salvation masochism has ever known

HOLLOWeen

A night of debauchery
        contemporary larceny
crime art~
        the most beautiful struggle
        painted in liberty's name

we're talking
        intoxicated canvases

we're talking
    pink flamingos dancing on rooftops
      mailboxes puking on lawns
          trespassing garden gnomes
            and toilette paper weeping willows

we're talking
        trick or treat
    with no sweet tooth

we're talking
        laugh at their pain
because *we can't hold ours up*

this rebel fist
is not in the name of revolution
it is a strike in the dark
hoping to feel something

this rebel cry
no call for change
just a thrust for attention
because on hollow days

validation is Almond Joy
    and there's already enough cavities unfilled
feed us with Kisses
love us even with our cavities
  even with our melancholy

we are masterpieces, you know
splattered and stained with imperfection
we are artwork, you know

hollow as we may be
we are liberty's struggle
    and we will keep our fist raised
        and our cries loud
until we are seen
        or heard
we will keep laughing
  that is the only time we feel alive

4 Corners

There is elegance in midnight
in moonshine and black light
in crow fights and dark dawns
in peons and low pawns
how shaded are the thick trees
how jaded are the bent knees
   or the bent wrists
     of the interests
       of the black fists
   in the sky
how downcast are the eyes
   of the voice of still I rise
how high is the rise
    of the voice of still I cry...

his face
   is bedtime empty
   with black hole Ray-Bans
he has seen the destruction of universes
   before they expand
on a street
   between 2 avenues
he has expanded to 4 corners
   exponential growth
    tends to happen s l o w e   r
where he's from
his vacuums
have sucked up 8 bloodbaths
and he is only 16
grey matter
cannot fathom age 32

or pension at 64
　　where he's from
keys do not open doors
　　　　there is force and deceit
　　　　　force and deceit
　　　　and love
is somewhere in the middle
prancing with a cat and a fiddle
as a cow
grazes on dreams
　　and so it seems
that he's a little 'black' around the edges
　　that he's 'black' with despair
　　　　that he's 'black' with hopelessness
　but his face is bedtime empty
and there is still innocence to his nursery rhyme
like Jack and Jill fucked raw
before they went up that hill
before they went to get that pale
before they went to get that pill
　　he is history
disguised as Dr. Seuss lines
　　a timeline
simplified to a misunderstood circle
　　　　and yet he failed math way before Geometry
if only you could see it from his angle
　　there is decadence in his perspective
　　but elegance in his struggle
　　　　he is still rising

A Literal Alliteration

My God!?!?
How much symbolism did you put in that thing?
From the looks of it, it's about to explode with over meaning!
Don't you know the rules of writing?
Didn't anyone ever tell you the cautionary tale of

~the hyperbolized metaphor~

how its author
got so lost in exaggeration
he couldn't find his way out
  whirling
          in the oblivion of a million black holes
they say Krishna swallowed him whole
never did find his bones
all the better
he wasn't an advocate of structure
used similes like loose change
  only when the big metaphors ran out
how ironic
that he worked for big government most of his life
counting and recounting his salary
with a frown

there are liberties in writing
found nowhere else
but there is still an economy of words
a literal alliteration aligning allotments of consonants and vowels
it's a bit oxymoronic but

too much of something can diminish the value
so remember
    the next time you're devising a poem
                                    short story
        novelette
                          novel
epic
           blog
                                        comic strip

      WHAT HAVE YOU!

there are many weapons in your arsenal
but *there is* such a thing as overkill

Washington Square Park

Does she know she's walking to the beat?
drums jazzing it up
   fountain sprinkling in her wake
a protest crashes her photoshoot
   and demands the air
while across the crowd, a harmonica chimes in
snare still aflare
   a child scampers into frame
     with a skateboarder at her heels

All of this in one Square
   a hub of art and creativity
a class of geniuses graduated here
as stoners sparked in one corner
and Fischers baited checkmate in another
there is love on the lawn
and graffiti on the concrete
the benches are littered with conversation and reflection

As night gives way to serenity
I wish this park never closed
that the guitar chords sang through dusk
and the fountain danced into dawn

My Father's Son

the ceiling is as conscious as I
on this very night
   I am my father's son
bottles litter the floor
                   the table
         the sink
their spirits are seeping in
this haunted vessel of mine
is no better than an empty room
           and now the streets?
   there are still bottles yet
I can hear them jingle as I walk
       can I ever escape their whaling
        incessant banshee cries
  in my sleep
I can see the gold labels
but they're not nightmares
  more like long lost friends
              calling out
I reach for them
   for the ceiling
only then do I realize
         I'm drowning

Building Babel

eyes in the sky
  and hands building Babel
he is as high as God
lost his sense of equilibrium
    when cents became dollars
        when knowledge became power

his future
       is a skyscraper built on clouds
     no staircase or elevator
with faith mounted on a wingtip
he has soared rivers
left behind wastelands
    and forgotten deserts

he lives in a penthouse
high above the *Antz*
A Bug's Life was a childhood ago
now he's the eye behind the glass

but on July 11th
he lost a love
I thank God for death - the great equalizer
for it keeps life in check

     on October 29th
     he lost power
     he lost power and all his cars
     and I thank God for disasters
     they level not only buildings but egos

just as gravity works against all

let tragedies hold us dear to humanity
let canceled flights remind us of Icarus

we are all feathers of a single bird
      but when we think ourselves rockets
      airborne in solitary
the wax melts
and we find ourselves in oblivion
staring up at the clouds from the pits of oceans

eyes in darkness
maybe he was building Babel
but now he's found Atlantis
yet another island lost at sea

The Circle of Life

Life cycles in revolution
do not get caught staring

Life cycles in revolution
do not get caught staring

Life cycles in revolution
do not get caught staring

the mind latches onto patterns
comfort. stability. familiarity
cyclical circles are hypnotizing
   but you are not meant to end where you started
the goal
is not to revolve around a single point
mindfuck the cogs
         into randomness
         into chaos
you do not fit into life's little crevices
                        Expand. Dilate. Grow
grow until you are too robust to handle
         create new spirals
   spiral out of control

there are things
         you will not notice about this world
   until you are off its axis
so be radical
   radically radiant
you choose the radius
just don't get caught in the cycle of it all
don't get caught staring

Ruby Bridges

I heard that you were shot

no, that wasn't you...

then why are you lying in a pool of blame
framing yourself in melanin

I heard that you were enslaved

oh, that wasn't you either...

then why are there whips of hatred across your back
animosity seared into your skin

I heard that the white man got his foot on your neck

let me guess, wasn't you...

then why are you so pain obsessed?

I, too, saw through Ruby's eyes
but that was 60 years ago
and I'm only 20 years young
those bridges have long been crossed
   though not yet burned
do not burden me with hatred
      I was not born of it
feed me my history
   but leave out all that self-pity
I do not like its texture
   it does not go down smooth with progress
Barack
   was in the house
      and before him was Rice
         and before her was Powell

tell me,
   who taught you to play the victim so well
it almost looks like the gun's not in your hands
spraying worldstars on ghetto corners
when will black on black not refer to crime
when will black on black not refer to crime

come on brothas
   share the love
c'mon cuzz
   spread the peace

I just want to mention that I've only been mugged once and it was by four brothas who called me cuzz like we were family but that's no way to bond

for me
   brotherhood stretches across race
I have 'bros' from high school
   and we get white boy wasted together
Yo tengo un hermano de El Salvador
   and we kick it like Pelé
I have an Indian thambi
   and we break bread over samosas

                              the world is not black and white
        the world is not black or white
                  the world is not some 50 shades of gray

            it is refracting rainbows and peacock feathers
                  it is white horse and black tar

it is sugar and spice
all jammed into an electrical socket
the sparks-
are every race, creed, and color
each with the potential to burn
   like arson
        or a lightbulb

either way, they can burn bridges
and though it's too late to change Ruby's past
there is still time for the future
do not burden it with hatred
all it needs is love

Election Year

a donkey fighting an elephant
seems a ridiculous notion
yet every four years, the ass brays
and the elephant trumpets

a parade filling more seats than the MGM Grand
a masquerade filling the eyes of the masses with sand
this star spangled lie infused dream of yore
lobbying with picket signs outside your door
lobbying with picket signs in front of your face

this race, this farce
this race, this sham
this race, this dream
this carrot dangling just out of reach
this *land that never has been yet, and yet must be*

the road paved with good intentions leads the same place
as that demon in your ear
from the wolf's howl into the jaws of the fox
death is inevitable
but you choose your fade to black

wipe that sand out of your eyes
see the wasteland that grew from these shores

WAKE UP

don't let them put lies in your head

WAKE UP

inception is just brays and trumpets
and marching bands are just noise to cover the whispers
all the demons conspiring behind locked doors
the wolves and the foxes plotting their next meal

WAKE UP

that noise is your alarm clock
America is not the greatest country in the world

but sure, let the donkey and the elephant fight
it is just as ridiculous as it sounds
just turn off the volume to the bullshit

*Langston Hughes Quote

But He Smoked Weed

Sirens remind me of the Amerikan flag:
of the hope lost between the stars
  of the white stripes

  those who surrender before the bloodshed
  those who surrender in the midst of bloodshed
  those who are shed before they understand surrender

HANDS UP, DON'T SHOOT!

we are the black
  overlooked in all the white
we are the red
  that keeps the concrete pumping
pumped with lead
  let this pencil be loud enough
    let this poem be loud enough

NO JUSTICE, NO PEACE!

pieced together
this Amerikan puzzle has always been disfigured
a bag of skittles left in the sun too long
we are a dream deferred

A Train - Uptown

I sat in a cypher of minds
beatboxing with insanity
listening to words vibrate off lensless glasses

they got you trapped in capitalism, my nigga

runaway slave sprinting on treadmills
         you ain't going nowhere
nowhere they don't want you
you think 1984 is the future
that shit was bred in your grandma's placenta
fed off lacerations curled around this nation

life is a trap, my nigga, and you fell for it

let me school you for a sec
come and scat
    with the fat cats

you've been whipped
but don't be ashamed
society has a strong grip
try to escape it by dressing different
but you're still the same nigga
chained to a gang of tap dancers
keep dancing, my nigga
hustlin' for fool's gold
keep that jive smile, my nigga

but we in Harlem
    twisted
and we know the truth

unscrew potential and find a tunnel from the ocean to the sky
my nigga, we infinite
living in sleeping eights
        we got the itis

ain't never waking from this Amerikan Dream
where money is cream
        and sugar
and they got you extra caffeinated
Malcolm X Blvd is where they breed revolutionaries and martyrs
tell 'em
        keep your mouth open
        and your mind closed
we'll wean you on Olympus Thunderbolts

you don't want that early rose so
        preach sanity
  preach rational
        preach possible
all that other shit is outside the beat
and you can't tap dance without rhythm
Blackface taught us that

Rubik's Cube

After a day's work:
return home, twist a cube for a couple of hours, then sleep.

We all live in a paradox
   contemplate the bigger picture and our place in it
   contemplate paradigm shifts and our place in it
years of thought have brought me to a solution
but what does it matter
       I don't understand it
what does it matter
       if I'm colorblind

The Gavel's End

CNN already has my eulogy
I'll die with it in my pocket
along with a snapshot of 12 year old magic
   the best shot ever taken
had all the angles
   and the hope of a buzzer beater
but buzzers sound like gavels
they echo in silence
reverberate with the same vigor as glory day games
    just more final

recurring nightmares with no visual
only justice
banging down the walls of sanity
you-
    trying to convince yourself you're a whole person
because Amerika's fractions don't add up
me-
    trying to convince myself my voice matters
when all my ideas are history
  and we're still spinning

a man was lynched tomorrow
and amid all the fire and tears
   the tree keeps standing
the rope still hasn't been seen
the protests last as long as a last breath
   recycled sentiments in rehashed hashtags
    remixed hymns in dejavu rally cries

WAIT!

flip back a couple pages
we already read this story
   we already asked that question
      tried that method
         wrote that history
still, the tree stands
death pinched me again today
and I think she's got a fetish with my skin
      the way it feels
   or moves
      or glows
so I leave home with a eulogy in my pocket
ready as if death is the loudest microphone my message will ever
have
hear me now:

    a history teacher once asked
    what do you know of justice
    and I responded
    that she's blind
    except when it comes to color
    that her scales tip right
    unless there is money involved
    that justice is a motherfucker
    do what she want, when she want
    and reports to no one
    she's the baddest bitch
    with more cover up than social filters

half the country with their head on a swivel
   half with their head in the clouds
too high to riot
   too scared to revolt
but in the midnight hour I swear the tree is laughing
premature fireworks taunting us to pop off
    maybe the only freedom we really have
oh, but I'll vote
I'll vote that we set this whole tree on fire
burn the leaves with the 3 branches
and constitute an ending to this sickness
riddle the trunk with bullets
until the crying sap tastes sweet
    I'll vote
that we blend the roots with eucalyptus
and swallow them whole
shit out the stars that were already blotted
    and start anew

September 27th

wanna hear a joke…

today my girlfriend told me she doesn't like poetry
and I cracked
that means she doesn't like you
how can you not like self-expression?
she slashed, "It's pretentious when people try to be deep"

well,
I wanna be deep
I wanna be deep like the rivers
or like the "Roots" I watched in 5th grade
I wanna be deep like my dick has never been
I wanna be deep like the debts of an entire nation
but more than that
I wanna be deep like those books I never put the effort in

she uses big words like 'lexicon'
her meaning is lost on me whenever we talk
but now, I tell her this
I tell her,
this is my lexicon, my language
it is lost on those who don't put in the effort
she loves those books
do you think she understands that I love you
that conjunctions don't conform to rules when we're together
that when I skip _____
it's because I'm leaving a gap for someone to fall into
when my wordplay is just playful
and flowers are there just for scent
do you think she knows that my pollen gives bees purpose
that even in a lost meaning, there can be beauty

we still haven't found our meaning
but we are beautiful

The Agnostic

I haven't prayed in years
  but last night
I felt a crease in my knees
  a steeple in my hands
    broken
I folded into the only temple I know
a mental crevice reserved for self-defense
when self-offenses get the best of heart
heart,
  you can be so weak sometimes
    or maybe
  there is just too much pressure on you
to bleed your rivers through the body
  and channel the constant flood of emotions
 it makes no damn sense
what keeps you pumping?
        there is an impulsive brain
        syn-asking you to stop
I sometimes wish you'd listen
crumple walls and just bleed out

the temple doors are open now
who will pray for me

Deliberation on Eden

When I eat apples
  I eat them whole
swallow everything except the stem
    let the core
      scrape against the ridges of my esophagus
let the seeds
float with the undercurrent of my belly
      they plant themselves
in cavernous depths
  yearning to be forgotten
    striving for it
and as I grow
  they grow too
sprouting in me the evils I was destined for
    there is an Adam's apple
lodged into the walls of my throat
it touches every word I speak
      hissing undertones of malevolence
I love you
  becomes a profession of lust
You're amazing
  a compliment laced with envy
the 7 deadlies are within me
but I cannot imagine them stemming from apples
you mean to tell me,
  my core has been rotting since I was a seed
swallow me down and let's see what grows between us

DiSaStEr

like the morning after, she is disaster
a juice carton
shake well
no time for the freshly squeezed
just add water
she is that morning fluff
      that always lulls me back to sleep
that sunshine smile shaded with toothpaste

BUT I STILL TASTE THE LUST

we will burn in hell for our gluttony
sizzling on the skillet with the swine
      that
           is our just dessert
this international breakfast our only reward
I have drowned in her chocolate far too many times
maybe,
      maybe if we added whipped cream we could be sweet
scrambled together by that cheesy Hollywood romance
we have become   a   natural   disaster
a juice carton
shaken well
we are mimosas
sobriety would never allow us
but in darkness
      we clawed homes of each other's arms
carved shelters of each other's ribs
we are eggshells
two yolks that never should have mixed

I must confess

my profession of love was never true
yet another lie I told her
because those syrupy midnights were my sugar high
but just like the sticky aftermath
we must be cleansed
we should have ended before we began

I am disaster
a juice carton
pour well

The Day is Old*

They call me present hedonistic
I don't let the crumbs of today's meals compile
I merely brush them to the floor
leftover chips aren't for bargaining wars
I go all in every night

Once shown a glimpse of my future
it was hazy
I guess I'm just near-sighted
see, my life is a roller coaster
like. every. body. else's
but full of orgasmic highs
the screams I've heard alone could make you orgasm
I understand that you live for tomorrow
but tomorrow is never promised
unbirthed daybreaks are a wishful dream
and abortion rates are high
deathshots ring through midnight
so yes...
I put all my eggs in the same basket
at least I can see here
  I can see now
you idolize hope
but deal daily in despair
my hope is in instants
  instant gratification
    mortification is unknown to me
I act before I think
because fear is a thought
and life is meant to be lived
not procrastinated

They call me prude
I'm always thinking about tomorrow
I don't see life as obstacles or
hindrances to better life
life for premature babies, they call me mother
death at my feet
I pick up this bag of bones and begin to walk
kissing new life as if we were lovers
distant but familiar soulmates
tonguing down canals of new hope

They call me life
rewind back
I understand where my past was rooted
color diverged into verbal genocide
were we even supposed to be here
eyes dilated from false substances
   how do you differentiate
    false gods
   or
  wishful thinking
clocks with forgotten time
take shackles off your mind
allow time to heal world's wounds
 each day
is last breathe in battered corpse
taking chances is the belief that God still exists

This is all just time
through dyslexic eyes
past footsteps
  swept by future winds

airy in the breeze
quick to sway from the unknown

Let your present be concrete sandcastles
but know
there is always room for renovations
we build to be broken down
so we lay sturdy foundations
Past   Present   Future
this is all just time
moments are what you make of them

*Co-written with Breanna Walker

The Third Rail

Not everyone is as sharp as you
as to the point as you
if I faint at the sight of blood
what good is your touch for my purposes
I am no masochist
I am not looking for a complicated relationship
my past is plagued with enough scabs
they are the reason I search for release

II.
My hands are not sturdy enough for such a burden
there is a reason I do not operate heavy machinery
when we caress
no good will come of it
such a lethal combination
our children would be explosive
a litany of gunpowder
but I stopped praying so long ago
I have forgotten the silence of God
I do not want a bullet
to enter the temple on my behalf

III.
My ancestors endured you in my stead
your symbolism
is too much for me to choke down
a long-term affair with poplars and strange fruit
I am too ripe to be hanging around you
no matter how much you unfurl yourself
we will never be compatible
you are a slow killer
and my breaths are full

IV.
If all your friends jumped off a bridge
would you do it too?
   I repeat
if **all** your friends jumped off a bridge
would you do it too?

V.
They say pain is to be ingested- like you
depression is to be ingested- like you
that is,
swallowed down and submerged
drowned into a dream like eternal
but you stopped being a solution for anxiety years ago
what makes you think you are a solution to life
when the sheep are done counting
and I'm done hopping fences
I will still be too woke for you

VI.
You are my buzzkill
the neon light drawing me in
for one glorious touch
rumors say you're electric
shocking to be exact
I was hoping you could enlighten me
be my pathway to the third eye
   I just want to shine

Life of a Tree

Have you ever looked up through a tree's network of branches and wondered...

How long did it take you to get up there?
Are your roots as endless as your branches?
Has your backbone always been so sturdy, or has it been tested?
      Bent to the ground by harsh storms before being deemed strong
Did the other little trees use to poke fun at you for that low hanging limb?
Did grandfather tree cast his shadow on you, instructing you in proper growth?
Or was he cut down before his time?
Did mother nature and father time do a rain dance to ensure that you were nurtured?
      As you ascended above the newborns,
did it ever occur to you that maybe they needed shade
  or someone to look up to?
Have you ever reached back down to touch another tree's life?
Or perhaps to drop a seed of wisdom?
      Do you ever ponder the meaning of your existence?
Or do you merely bask in the fact that you have the opportunity to ponder?
If I told you, you were to be struck down tomorrow,
would you look back through your inner rings in melancholy?
Would sap roll down your trunk in streams of sadness?
Or would you stand **bolder** than ever before, in righteous pride?

Mr. Tree, Ms. Tree
Are you proud of the leaves you've shed?
The seasons you've endured?
Are you proud of your legacy?

Acknowledgements

A great deal of appreciation goes out to my support network of family and friends. Your perspectives and consistent words of encouragement made this vision into a reality.

To my mom, thank you for your unconditional love and never-ending cheerleading.

To my chosen family: Wes, Breanna, Allan, Lis, Pablo, Priscilla, Karl and Brittany- thank you for the substance and value you have continued to pour into me over the years.

To the greater poetry community, thank you for your effervescent pens and continuous inspiration to improve my craft and share.

Made in the USA
Middletown, DE
16 January 2021